MW01714362

The Awesome Fisherman's Fishing Log Book: A Journal For Anglers To Record And Track Fishing Trips And Catch Statistics

Dubreck World Publishing

Copyright

'The Awesome Fisherman's Fishing Log Book: A Journal For Anglers To Record And Track Fishing Trips And Catch Statistics'

First published in August 2021 by Dubreck World Publishing
Printed and bound by Lulu Press
Distributed by Lulu Press

ISBN-13: 978-1-312-31224-1
First Edition

DUBRECK WORLD PUBLISHING

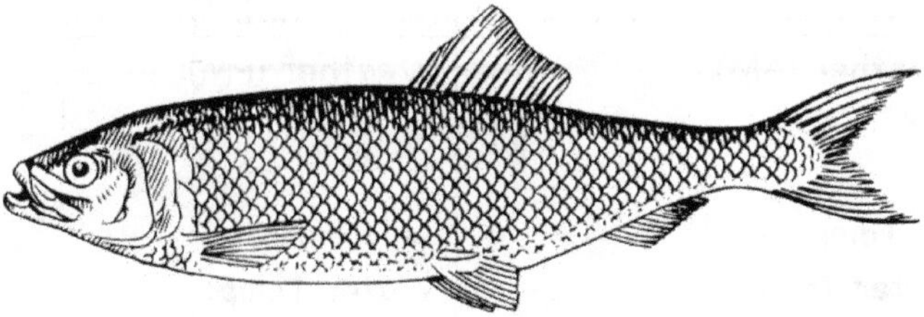

Dedicated to all
Awesome anglers
Young and old!

If found, please return to:

....

Date:……………………….Location:…………………………………..

Companions:………………………………………………………………..

……………………………………………………………………………………….

Weather (AM):	Weather (PM):
Air Temp: Water Temp: Wind Speed: Wind Direction:	Air Temp: Water Temp: Wind Speed: Wind Direction:

Moon: ● ◐ ◐ ◯ ◯ ◯ ◑ ◑

Water Clarity:

Water Level: High ☐ Low ☐ Midway ☐

Fishing Rod / Reel:
Bait:
Lures:
Rig:
Fishing Method:

Notes

Species	Length	Weight	Girth

Largest Catch: Species:

Length: Weight: Girth:

Total Fish Caught:

Date:……………………….Location:………………………………….
Companions:……………………………………………………………….
…………………………………………………………………………………….

Weather (AM):	Weather (PM):
Air Temp: Water Temp: Wind Speed: Wind Direction:	Air Temp: Water Temp: Wind Speed: Wind Direction:

Moon: ● ◐ ◐ ◯ ◯ ◯ ◑ ◑

Water Clarity:
Water Level: High ☐ Low ☐ Midway ☐

Fishing Rod / Reel:
Bait:
Lures:
Rig:
Fishing Method:

Notes

Species	Length	Weight	Girth

Largest Catch: Species:

Length: Weight: Girth:

Total Fish Caught:

Date:……………………….Location:………………………………….

Companions:…………………………………………………………….

……………………………………………………………………………….

Weather (AM): Air Temp: Water Temp: Wind Speed: Wind Direction:	Weather (PM): Air Temp: Water Temp: Wind Speed: Wind Direction:

Moon: ● ◐ ◐ ◯ ◯ ◯ ◑ ◑

Water Clarity:
Water Level: High ☐ Low ☐ Midway ☐

Fishing Rod / Reel:
Bait:
Lures:
Rig:
Fishing Method:

Notes

Species	Length	Weight	Girth

Largest Catch: Species:

Length: Weight: Girth:

Total Fish Caught:

Date:……………………….Location:…………………………………

Companions:……………………………………………………………………

……………………………………………………………………………………

Weather (AM):	Weather (PM):
Air Temp:	Air Temp:
Water Temp:	Water Temp:
Wind Speed:	Wind Speed:
Wind Direction:	Wind Direction:

Moon: ● ◐ ◐ ◯ ◯ ◯ ◑ ◑

Water Clarity:			
Water Level:	High ☐	Low ☐	Midway ☐

Fishing Rod / Reel:
Bait:
Lures:
Rig:
Fishing Method:

Notes

____

____

____

____

Species	Length	Weight	Girth

Largest Catch: Species:

Length: Weight: Girth:

Total Fish Caught:

Date:……………………….Location:…………………………………

Companions:………………………………………………………………

………………………………………………………………………………

Weather (AM):	Weather (PM):
Air Temp: Water Temp: Wind Speed: Wind Direction:	Air Temp: Water Temp: Wind Speed: Wind Direction:

Moon:

Water Clarity:
Water Level: High ☐ Low ☐ Midway ☐

Fishing Rod / Reel:
Bait:
Lures:
Rig:
Fishing Method:

Notes

Species	Length	Weight	Girth

<u>Largest Catch:</u> Species:

Length: Weight: Girth:

Total Fish Caught:

Date:……………………….Location:……………………………….

Companions:……………………………………………………….

……………………………………………………………………….

Weather (AM):	Weather (PM):
Air Temp:	Air Temp:
Water Temp:	Water Temp:
Wind Speed:	Wind Speed:
Wind Direction:	Wind Direction:

Moon: ● ◐ ◐ ◯ ◯ ◯ ◑ ◑

Water Clarity:			
Water Level:	High ☐	Low ☐	Midway ☐

Fishing Rod / Reel:
Bait:
Lures:
Rig:
Fishing Method:

Notes

Species	Length	Weight	Girth

Largest Catch: Species:

Length: Weight: Girth:

Total Fish Caught:

Date:……………………….Location:……………………………….

Companions:……………………………………………………………….

……………………………………………………………………………………….

Weather (AM):	Weather (PM):
Air Temp:	Air Temp:
Water Temp:	Water Temp:
Wind Speed:	Wind Speed:
Wind Direction:	Wind Direction:

Moon:

Water Clarity:	
Water Level:	High ☐ Low ☐ Midway ☐

Fishing Rod / Reel:	
Bait:	
Lures:	
Rig:	
Fishing Method:	

Notes

Species	Length	Weight	Girth

Largest Catch: Species:

Length: Weight: Girth:

Total Fish Caught:

Date:……………………….Location:……………………………….

Companions:……………………………………………………………….

……………………………………………………………………………….

Weather (AM):	Weather (PM):
Air Temp:	Air Temp:
Water Temp:	Water Temp:
Wind Speed:	Wind Speed:
Wind Direction:	Wind Direction:

Moon: ● ◐ ◐ ◯ ◯ ◯ ◑ ◑

Water Clarity:	
Water Level:	High ☐ Low ☐ Midway ☐

Fishing Rod / Reel:
Bait:
Lures:
Rig:
Fishing Method:

Notes

Species	Length	Weight	Girth

Largest Catch: Species:

Length: Weight: Girth:

Total Fish Caught:

Date:……………………….Location:…………………………………

Companions:……………………………………………………………

…………………………………………………………………………………

Weather (AM): Air Temp: Water Temp: Wind Speed: Wind Direction:	Weather (PM): Air Temp: Water Temp: Wind Speed: Wind Direction:

Moon: ● ◐ ◐ ◐ ○ ◑ ◑ ◑

Water Clarity: Water Level: High ☐ Low ☐ Midway ☐

Fishing Rod / Reel:
Bait:
Lures:
Rig:
Fishing Method:

Notes

Species	Length	Weight	Girth

Largest Catch: Species:

Length: Weight: Girth:

Total Fish Caught:

Date:………………………Location:………………………………

Companions:………………………………………………………………

……………………………………………………………………………………

Weather (AM):	Weather (PM):
Air Temp:	Air Temp:
Water Temp:	Water Temp:
Wind Speed:	Wind Speed:
Wind Direction:	Wind Direction:

Moon: ● ◐ ◐ ◯ ○ ◯ ◑ ◑

Water Clarity:

Water Level: High ☐ Low ☐ Midway ☐

Fishing Rod / Reel:	
Bait:	
Lures:	
Rig:	
Fishing Method:	

Notes

Species	Length	Weight	Girth

Largest Catch: Species:

Length: Weight: Girth:

Total Fish Caught:

Date:…………………………….Location:…………………………………….

Companions:………………………………………………………………….

…………………………………………………………………………………….

Weather (AM):	Weather (PM):
Air Temp:	Air Temp:
Water Temp:	Water Temp:
Wind Speed:	Wind Speed:
Wind Direction:	Wind Direction:

Moon: ● ◐ ◐ ◐ ○ ◑ ◑ ◑

Water Clarity:			
Water Level:	High ☐	Low ☐	Midway ☐

Fishing Rod / Reel:
Bait:
Lures:
Rig:
Fishing Method:

Notes

Species	Length	Weight	Girth

Largest Catch: Species:

Length: Weight: Girth:

Total Fish Caught:

Date:……………………………Location:……………………………………

Companions:……………………………………………………………………

……………………………………………………………………………………

Weather (AM):	Weather (PM):
Air Temp:	Air Temp:
Water Temp:	Water Temp:
Wind Speed:	Wind Speed:
Wind Direction:	Wind Direction:

Moon: ● ◐ ◐ ◐ ○ ◑ ◑ ◑

Water Clarity:
Water Level: High ☐ Low ☐ Midway ☐

Fishing Rod / Reel:
Bait:
Lures:
Rig:
Fishing Method:

Notes

Species	Length	Weight	Girth

Largest Catch: Species:

Length: Weight: Girth:

Total Fish Caught:

Date:………………………Location:……………………………….

Companions:…………………………………………………………….

……………………………………………………………………………….

Weather (AM):	Weather (PM):
Air Temp:	Air Temp:
Water Temp:	Water Temp:
Wind Speed:	Wind Speed:
Wind Direction:	Wind Direction:

Moon: ● ◐ ◐ ◯ ◯ ◯ ◑ ◑

Water Clarity:
Water Level: High ☐ Low ☐ Midway ☐

Fishing Rod / Reel:
Bait:
Lures:
Rig:
Fishing Method:

Notes

____

____

____

____

Species	Length	Weight	Girth

Largest Catch: Species:

Length: Weight: Girth:

Total Fish Caught:

Date:………………………….Location:…………………………………….

Companions:……………………………………………………………………….

……………………………………………………………………………………………….

Weather (AM):	Weather (PM):
Air Temp:	Air Temp:
Water Temp:	Water Temp:
Wind Speed:	Wind Speed:
Wind Direction:	Wind Direction:

Moon: ● ◐ ◐ ◯ ◯ ◑ ◑ ◑

Water Clarity:

Water Level: High ☐ Low ☐ Midway ☐

Fishing Rod / Reel:
Bait:
Lures:
Rig:
Fishing Method:

Notes

____

____

____

____

Species	Length	Weight	Girth

Largest Catch: Species:

Length: Weight: Girth:

Total Fish Caught:

Date:……………………….Location:……………………………….

Companions:……………………………………………………………….

……………………………………………………………………………….

Weather (AM):	Weather (PM):
Air Temp:	Air Temp:
Water Temp:	Water Temp:
Wind Speed:	Wind Speed:
Wind Direction:	Wind Direction:

Moon: ● ◐ ◐ ◯ ◯ ◯ ◑ ◑

Water Clarity:			
Water Level:	High ☐	Low ☐	Midway ☐

Fishing Rod / Reel:
Bait:
Lures:
Rig:
Fishing Method:

Notes

Species	Length	Weight	Girth

Largest Catch: Species:

Length: Weight: Girth:

Total Fish Caught:

Date:………………………….Location:……………………………………….

Companions:……………………………………………………………………….

……………………………………………………………………………………………

Weather (AM):	Weather (PM):
Air Temp: Water Temp: Wind Speed: Wind Direction:	Air Temp: Water Temp: Wind Speed: Wind Direction:

Moon:

Water Clarity:

Water Level: High ☐ Low ☐ Midway ☐

Fishing Rod / Reel:
Bait:
Lures:
Rig:
Fishing Method:

Notes

Species	Length	Weight	Girth

Largest Catch: Species:

Length: Weight: Girth:

Total Fish Caught:

Date:…………………………Location:……………………………………

Companions:……………………………………………………………………

……………………………………………………………………………………………

Weather (AM):	Weather (PM):
Air Temp: Water Temp: Wind Speed: Wind Direction:	Air Temp: Water Temp: Wind Speed: Wind Direction:

Moon: ● ◐ ◐ ☾ ○ ☽ ◑ ◑

Water Clarity:

Water Level: High ☐ Low ☐ Midway ☐

Fishing Rod / Reel:
Bait:
Lures:
Rig:
Fishing Method:

Notes

Species	Length	Weight	Girth

Largest Catch: Species:

Length: Weight: Girth:

Total Fish Caught:

Date:……………………….Location:……………………………….

Companions:……………………………………………………………….

……………………………………………………………………………………

Weather (AM): Air Temp: Water Temp: Wind Speed: Wind Direction:	Weather (PM): Air Temp: Water Temp: Wind Speed: Wind Direction:

Moon: ● ◐ ◐ ◯ ◯ ◯ ◑ ◑

Water Clarity:
Water Level: High ☐ Low ☐ Midway ☐

Fishing Rod / Reel:
Bait:
Lures:
Rig:
Fishing Method:

Notes

Species	Length	Weight	Girth

Largest Catch: Species:

Length: Weight: Girth:

Total Fish Caught:

Date:………………………Location:………………………………

Companions:………………………………………………………………

…………………………………………………………………………………

Weather (AM):	Weather (PM):
Air Temp:	Air Temp:
Water Temp:	Water Temp:
Wind Speed:	Wind Speed:
Wind Direction:	Wind Direction:

Moon: ● ◐ ◐ ☾ ○ ☽ ◑ ◑

Water Clarity:			
Water Level:	High ☐	Low ☐	Midway ☐

Fishing Rod / Reel:
Bait:
Lures:
Rig:
Fishing Method:

Notes

Species	Length	Weight	Girth

<u>Largest Catch:</u> Species:

Length: Weight: Girth:

Total Fish Caught:

Date:……………………….Location:…………………………………

Companions:…………………………………………………………………

…………………………………………………………………………………

Weather (AM):	Weather (PM):
Air Temp:	Air Temp:
Water Temp:	Water Temp:
Wind Speed:	Wind Speed:
Wind Direction:	Wind Direction:

Moon: ● ◐ ◐ ◯ ◯ ◯ ◑ ◑

Water Clarity:			
Water Level:	High ☐	Low ☐	Midway ☐

Fishing Rod / Reel:
Bait:
Lures:
Rig:
Fishing Method:

Notes

Species	Length	Weight	Girth

<u>Largest Catch:</u> Species:

Length: Weight: Girth:

Total Fish Caught:

Date:……………………….Location:……………………………….

Companions:……………………………………………………….

……………………………………………………………………………

Weather (AM):	Weather (PM):
Air Temp:	Air Temp:
Water Temp:	Water Temp:
Wind Speed:	Wind Speed:
Wind Direction:	Wind Direction:

Moon:

Water Clarity:

Water Level: High ☐ Low ☐ Midway ☐

Fishing Rod / Reel:
Bait:
Lures:
Rig:
Fishing Method:

Notes

Species	Length	Weight	Girth

<u>Largest Catch:</u> Species:

Length: Weight: Girth:

Total Fish Caught:

Date:…………………………Location:………………………………….
Companions:……………………………………………………………….

……………………………………………………………………………………….

Weather (AM):	Weather (PM):
Air Temp: Water Temp: Wind Speed: Wind Direction:	Air Temp: Water Temp: Wind Speed: Wind Direction:

Moon: ● ◐ ◐ ☾ ○ ☽ ◑ ◑

Water Clarity:
Water Level: High ☐ Low ☐ Midway ☐

Fishing Rod / Reel:
Bait:
Lures:
Rig:
Fishing Method:

Notes

Species	Length	Weight	Girth

Largest Catch: Species:

Length: Weight: Girth:

Total Fish Caught:

Date:……………………….Location:……………………………….
Companions:……………………………………………………………….
……………………………………………………………………………………….

Weather (AM):	Weather (PM):
Air Temp: Water Temp: Wind Speed: Wind Direction:	Air Temp: Water Temp: Wind Speed: Wind Direction:

Moon: ● ◐ ◐ ◯ ◯ ◯ ◑ ◑

Water Clarity:
Water Level: High ☐ Low ☐ Midway ☐

Fishing Rod / Reel:
Bait:
Lures:
Rig:
Fishing Method:

Notes

Species	Length	Weight	Girth

Largest Catch: Species:

Length: Weight: Girth:

Total Fish Caught:

Date:........................Location:..................................

Companions:...

....

Weather (AM):	Weather (PM):
Air Temp: Water Temp: Wind Speed: Wind Direction:	Air Temp: Water Temp: Wind Speed: Wind Direction:

Moon: ● ◐ ◐ ◯ ◯ ◯ ◑ ◑

Water Clarity:
Water Level: High ☐ Low ☐ Midway ☐

Fishing Rod / Reel:
Bait:
Lures:
Rig:
Fishing Method:

Notes

Species	Length	Weight	Girth

<u>Largest Catch:</u> Species:

Length: Weight: Girth:

Total Fish Caught:

Date:……………………….Location:……………………………….

Companions:…………………………………………………………….

……………………………………………………………………………….

Weather (AM):	Weather (PM):
Air Temp:	Air Temp:
Water Temp:	Water Temp:
Wind Speed:	Wind Speed:
Wind Direction:	Wind Direction:

Moon:

Water Clarity:
Water Level: High ☐ Low ☐ Midway ☐

Fishing Rod / Reel:
Bait:
Lures:
Rig:
Fishing Method:

Notes

Species	Length	Weight	Girth

Largest Catch: Species:

Length: Weight: Girth:

Total Fish Caught:

Date:………………………Location:………………………………

Companions:…………………………………………………………………

……………………………………………………………………………………

Weather (AM):	Weather (PM):
Air Temp:	Air Temp:
Water Temp:	Water Temp:
Wind Speed:	Wind Speed:
Wind Direction:	Wind Direction:

Moon: ● ◐ ◐ ◯ ◯ ◯ ◑ ◑

Water Clarity:			
Water Level:	High ☐	Low ☐	Midway ☐

Fishing Rod / Reel:
Bait:
Lures:
Rig:
Fishing Method:

Notes

Species	Length	Weight	Girth

Largest Catch: Species:

Length: Weight: Girth:

Total Fish Caught:

Date:……………………….Location:……………………………….

Companions:……………………………………………………….

…………………………………………………………………….

Weather (AM):	Weather (PM):
Air Temp: Water Temp: Wind Speed: Wind Direction:	Air Temp: Water Temp: Wind Speed: Wind Direction:

Moon: ● ◐ ◐ ◯ ◯ ◑ ◑ ◑

Water Clarity:
Water Level: High ☐ Low ☐ Midway ☐

Fishing Rod / Reel:
Bait:
Lures:
Rig:
Fishing Method:

Notes

Species	Length	Weight	Girth

Largest Catch: Species:

Length: Weight: Girth:

Total Fish Caught:

Date:……………………….Location:……………………………….

Companions:…………………………………………………………….

……………………………………………………………………………….

Weather (AM): Air Temp: Water Temp: Wind Speed: Wind Direction:	Weather (PM): Air Temp: Water Temp: Wind Speed: Wind Direction:

Moon: ● ◐ ◐ ◯ ◯ ◑ ◑ ◑

Water Clarity:

Water Level: High ☐ Low ☐ Midway ☐

Fishing Rod / Reel:
Bait:
Lures:
Rig:
Fishing Method:

Notes

Species	Length	Weight	Girth

Largest Catch: Species:

Length: Weight: Girth:

Total Fish Caught:

Date:……………………….Location:……………………………….

Companions:………………………………………………………….

…………………………………………………………………………….

Weather (AM): Air Temp: Water Temp: Wind Speed: Wind Direction:	Weather (PM): Air Temp: Water Temp: Wind Speed: Wind Direction:

Moon: ● ◐ ◐ ◐ ○ ◑ ◑ ◑

Water Clarity:
Water Level: High ☐ Low ☐ Midway ☐

Fishing Rod / Reel:
Bait:
Lures:
Rig:
Fishing Method:

Notes

Species	Length	Weight	Girth

<u>Largest Catch:</u> Species:

Length: Weight: Girth:

Total Fish Caught:

Date:……………………….Location:………………………………

Companions:…………………………………………………………

……………………………………………………………………………

Weather (AM): Air Temp: Water Temp: Wind Speed: Wind Direction:	Weather (PM): Air Temp: Water Temp: Wind Speed: Wind Direction:

Moon: ● ◐ ◐ ◯ ◯ ◯ ◑ ◑

Water Clarity:
Water Level: High ☐ Low ☐ Midway ☐

Fishing Rod / Reel:
Bait:
Lures:
Rig:
Fishing Method:

Notes

Species	Length	Weight	Girth

Largest Catch: Species:

Length: Weight: Girth:

Total Fish Caught:

Date:……………………….Location:………………………………….

Companions:…………………………………………………………….

…………………………………………………………………………….

Weather (AM):	Weather (PM):
Air Temp:	Air Temp:
Water Temp:	Water Temp:
Wind Speed:	Wind Speed:
Wind Direction:	Wind Direction:

Moon: ●◐◐◐○◑◑◑

Water Clarity:
Water Level: High ☐ Low ☐ Midway ☐

Fishing Rod / Reel:
Bait:
Lures:
Rig:
Fishing Method:

Notes

Species	Length	Weight	Girth

Largest Catch: Species:

Length: Weight: Girth:

Total Fish Caught:

Date:…………………………Location:…………………………………

Companions:………………………………………………………………

……………………………………………………………………………………

Weather (AM):	Weather (PM):
Air Temp:	Air Temp:
Water Temp:	Water Temp:
Wind Speed:	Wind Speed:
Wind Direction:	Wind Direction:

Moon: ● ◐ ◐ ◯ ○ ◯ ◑ ◑

Water Clarity:	
Water Level:	High ☐ Low ☐ Midway ☐

Fishing Rod / Reel:
Bait:
Lures:
Rig:
Fishing Method:

Notes

Species	Length	Weight	Girth

Largest Catch: Species:

Length: Weight: Girth:

Total Fish Caught:

Date:……………………….Location:………………………………..

Companions:………………………………………………………………

……………………………………………………………………………………

Weather (AM):	Weather (PM):
Air Temp:	Air Temp:
Water Temp:	Water Temp:
Wind Speed:	Wind Speed:
Wind Direction:	Wind Direction:

Moon: ● ◐ ◐ ◯ ○ ◯ ◑ ◑

Water Clarity:
Water Level: High ☐ Low ☐ Midway ☐

Fishing Rod / Reel:
Bait:
Lures:
Rig:
Fishing Method:

Notes

Species	Length	Weight	Girth

<u>Largest Catch:</u> Species:

Length: Weight: Girth:

Total Fish Caught:

Date:……………………….Location:………………………………

Companions:…………………………………………………………

………………………………………………………………………………

Weather (AM):	Weather (PM):
Air Temp: Water Temp: Wind Speed: Wind Direction:	Air Temp: Water Temp: Wind Speed: Wind Direction:

Moon: ● ◐ ◐ ◯ ○ ◯ ◑ ◑

Water Clarity:

Water Level: High ☐ Low ☐ Midway ☐

Fishing Rod / Reel:
Bait:
Lures:
Rig:
Fishing Method:

Notes

Species	Length	Weight	Girth

Largest Catch: Species:

Length: Weight: Girth:

Total Fish Caught:

Date:………………………Location:……………………………….

Companions:…………………………………………………………….

…………………………………………………………………………….

Weather (AM): Air Temp: Water Temp: Wind Speed: Wind Direction:	Weather (PM): Air Temp: Water Temp: Wind Speed: Wind Direction:

Moon: ● ◐ ◐ ◯ ◯ ◯ ◑ ◑ ●

Water Clarity:

Water Level: High ☐ Low ☐ Midway ☐

Fishing Rod / Reel:
Bait:
Lures:
Rig:
Fishing Method:

Notes

Species	Length	Weight	Girth

Largest Catch: Species:

Length: Weight: Girth:

Total Fish Caught:

Date:………………………….Location:…………………………………….

Companions:…………………………………………………………………….

…………………………………………………………………………………….

Weather (AM):	Weather (PM):
Air Temp: Water Temp: Wind Speed: Wind Direction:	Air Temp: Water Temp: Wind Speed: Wind Direction:

Moon: ● ◐ ◐ ◯ ◯ ◯ ◑ ◑

Water Clarity:

Water Level: High ☐ Low ☐ Midway ☐

Fishing Rod / Reel:
Bait:
Lures:
Rig:
Fishing Method:

Notes

Species	Length	Weight	Girth

Largest Catch: Species:

Length: Weight: Girth:

Total Fish Caught:

Date:……………………….Location:………………………………

Companions:………………………………………………………………

……………………………………………………………………………………

Weather (AM):	Weather (PM):
Air Temp: Water Temp: Wind Speed: Wind Direction:	Air Temp: Water Temp: Wind Speed: Wind Direction:

Moon: ● ◐ ◐ ◐ ○ ◑ ◑ ◑

Water Clarity:
Water Level: High ☐ Low ☐ Midway ☐

Fishing Rod / Reel:
Bait:
Lures:
Rig:
Fishing Method:

Notes

Species	Length	Weight	Girth

Largest Catch: Species:

Length: Weight: Girth:

Total Fish Caught:

Date:……………………….Location:……………………………….
Companions:…………………………………………………….

………………………………………………………………………….

Weather (AM):	Weather (PM):
Air Temp: Water Temp: Wind Speed: Wind Direction:	Air Temp: Water Temp: Wind Speed: Wind Direction:

Moon: ● ◐ ◐ ◯ ◯ ◯ ◑ ◑

Water Clarity:			
Water Level:	High ☐	Low ☐	Midway ☐

Fishing Rod / Reel:
Bait:
Lures:
Rig:
Fishing Method:

Notes

Species	Length	Weight	Girth

Largest Catch: Species:

Length: Weight: Girth:

Total Fish Caught:

Date:……………………….Location:……………………………….

Companions:……………………………………………………………….

……………………………………………………………………………………….

Weather (AM):	Weather (PM):
Air Temp:	Air Temp:
Water Temp:	Water Temp:
Wind Speed:	Wind Speed:
Wind Direction:	Wind Direction:

Moon: ● ◐ ◐ ◯ ○ ◯ ◑ ●

Water Clarity:			
Water Level:	High ☐	Low ☐	Midway ☐

Fishing Rod / Reel:
Bait:
Lures:
Rig:
Fishing Method:

Notes

Species	Length	Weight	Girth

Largest Catch: Species:

Length: Weight: Girth:

Total Fish Caught:

Date:…………………………Location:…………………………………

Companions:……………………………………………………………………

………………………………………………………………………………………

Weather (AM):	Weather (PM):
Air Temp: Water Temp: Wind Speed: Wind Direction:	Air Temp: Water Temp: Wind Speed: Wind Direction:

Moon: ● ◐ ◐ ◯ ◯ ◯ ◑ ◑

Water Clarity:
Water Level: High ☐ Low ☐ Midway ☐

Fishing Rod / Reel:
Bait:
Lures:
Rig:
Fishing Method:

Notes

Species	Length	Weight	Girth

Largest Catch: Species:

Length: Weight: Girth:

Total Fish Caught:

Date:…………………………Location:…………………………………

Companions:…………………………………………………………………

…………………………………………………………………………………………

Weather (AM):	Weather (PM):
Air Temp: Water Temp: Wind Speed: Wind Direction:	Air Temp: Water Temp: Wind Speed: Wind Direction:

Moon: ● ◐ ◐ ◯ ◯ ◯ ◑ ◑

Water Clarity:

Water Level: High ☐ Low ☐ Midway ☐

Fishing Rod / Reel:
Bait:
Lures:
Rig:
Fishing Method:

Notes

Species	Length	Weight	Girth

Largest Catch: Species:

Length: Weight: Girth:

Total Fish Caught:

Date:........................Location:..................................

Companions:..

....

Weather (AM):	Weather (PM):
Air Temp: Water Temp: Wind Speed: Wind Direction:	Air Temp: Water Temp: Wind Speed: Wind Direction:

Moon: ● ◐ ◐ ◯ ◯ ◯ ◑ ◑

Water Clarity:
Water Level: High ☐ Low ☐ Midway ☐

Fishing Rod / Reel:
Bait:
Lures:
Rig:
Fishing Method:

Notes

Species	Length	Weight	Girth

Largest Catch: Species:

Length: Weight: Girth:

Total Fish Caught:

Date:…………………………Location:……………………………………

Companions:…………………………………………………………………………

……………………………………………………………………………………………

Weather (AM):	Weather (PM):
Air Temp:	Air Temp:
Water Temp:	Water Temp:
Wind Speed:	Wind Speed:
Wind Direction:	Wind Direction:

Moon: ● ◐ ◐ ◯ ◯ ◑ ◑ ◑

Water Clarity:

Water Level: High ☐ Low ☐ Midway ☐

Fishing Rod / Reel:
Bait:
Lures:
Rig:
Fishing Method:

Notes

Species	Length	Weight	Girth

Largest Catch: Species:

Length: Weight: Girth:

Total Fish Caught:

Date:…………………………Location:……………………………………

Companions:……………………………………………………………………

……………………………………………………………………………………………

Weather (AM):	Weather (PM):
Air Temp: Water Temp: Wind Speed: Wind Direction:	Air Temp: Water Temp: Wind Speed: Wind Direction:

Moon: ● ◐ ◐ ◯ ◯ ◯ ◑ ◑

Water Clarity:

Water Level: High ☐ Low ☐ Midway ☐

Fishing Rod / Reel:
Bait:
Lures:
Rig:
Fishing Method:

Notes

Species	Length	Weight	Girth

Largest Catch: Species:

Length: Weight: Girth:

Total Fish Caught:

Date:…………………………Location:……………………………………

Companions:……………………………………………………………………

……………………………………………………………………………………………………

Weather (AM):	Weather (PM):
Air Temp: Water Temp: Wind Speed: Wind Direction:	Air Temp: Water Temp: Wind Speed: Wind Direction:

Moon: ● ◐ ◐ ◯ ◯ ◯ ◑ ◑

Water Clarity:
Water Level: High ☐ Low ☐ Midway ☐

Fishing Rod / Reel:
Bait:
Lures:
Rig:
Fishing Method:

Notes

Species	Length	Weight	Girth

Largest Catch: Species:

Length: Weight: Girth:

Total Fish Caught:

Date:…………………………Location:……………………………………

Companions:…………………………………………………………………………

…………………………………………………………………………………………

Weather (AM):	Weather (PM):
Air Temp:	Air Temp:
Water Temp:	Water Temp:
Wind Speed:	Wind Speed:
Wind Direction:	Wind Direction:

Moon: ● ◐ ◐ ☾ ○ ☽ ◑ ◑

Water Clarity:
Water Level: High ☐ Low ☐ Midway ☐

Fishing Rod / Reel:
Bait:
Lures:
Rig:
Fishing Method:

Notes

Species	Length	Weight	Girth

Largest Catch: Species:

Length: Weight: Girth:

Total Fish Caught:

Date:……………………….Location:…………………………………

Companions:………………………………………………………………….

…………………………………………………………………………………

Weather (AM): Air Temp: Water Temp: Wind Speed: Wind Direction:	Weather (PM): Air Temp: Water Temp: Wind Speed: Wind Direction:

Moon: ● ◐ ◐ ◯ ◯ ◯ ◑ ◑

Water Clarity:
Water Level: High ☐ Low ☐ Midway ☐

Fishing Rod / Reel:
Bait:
Lures:
Rig:
Fishing Method:

Notes

Species	Length	Weight	Girth

Largest Catch: Species:

Length: Weight: Girth:

Total Fish Caught:

Date:……………………….Location:……………………………….

Companions:………………………………………………………………

……………………………………………………………………………………

Weather (AM):	Weather (PM):
Air Temp: Water Temp: Wind Speed: Wind Direction:	Air Temp: Water Temp: Wind Speed: Wind Direction:

Moon: ● ◐ ◐ ◯ ◯ ◯ ◑ ◑

Water Clarity:

Water Level: High ☐ Low ☐ Midway ☐

Fishing Rod / Reel:
Bait:
Lures:
Rig:
Fishing Method:

Notes

Species	Length	Weight	Girth

Largest Catch: Species:

Length: Weight: Girth:

Total Fish Caught:

Date:…………………………….Location:……………………………………….
Companions:……………………………………………………………………….
……………………………………………………………………………………………

Weather (AM):	Weather (PM):
Air Temp: Water Temp: Wind Speed: Wind Direction:	Air Temp: Water Temp: Wind Speed: Wind Direction:

Moon: ● ◐ ◐ ◯ ◯ ◯ ◑ ◑

Water Clarity:

Water Level: High ☐ Low ☐ Midway ☐

Fishing Rod / Reel:
Bait:
Lures:
Rig:
Fishing Method:

Notes

Species	Length	Weight	Girth

Largest Catch: Species:

Length: Weight: Girth:

Total Fish Caught:

Date:……………………….Location:…………………………………

Companions:…………………………………………………………………

………………………………………………………………………………………

Weather (AM):	Weather (PM):
Air Temp:	Air Temp:
Water Temp:	Water Temp:
Wind Speed:	Wind Speed:
Wind Direction:	Wind Direction:

Moon: ● ◐ ◐ ☾ ○ ☽ ◑ ◑

Water Clarity:

Water Level: High ☐ Low ☐ Midway ☐

Fishing Rod / Reel:
Bait:
Lures:
Rig:
Fishing Method:

Notes

Species	Length	Weight	Girth

<u>Largest Catch:</u> Species:

Length: Weight: Girth:

Total Fish Caught:

Date:……………………….Location:………………………………….

Companions:…………………………………………………………………….

…………………………………………………………………………………….

Weather (AM):	Weather (PM):
Air Temp:	Air Temp:
Water Temp:	Water Temp:
Wind Speed:	Wind Speed:
Wind Direction:	Wind Direction:

Moon: ● ◐ ◐ ◯ ○ ◯ ◑ ◑

Water Clarity:	
Water Level:	High ☐ Low ☐ Midway ☐

Fishing Rod / Reel:
Bait:
Lures:
Rig:
Fishing Method:

Notes

Species	Length	Weight	Girth

Largest Catch: Species:

Length: Weight: Girth:

Total Fish Caught:

Date:………………………….Location:……………………………………

Companions:………………………………………………………………………

……………………………………………………………………………………………

Weather (AM):	Weather (PM):
Air Temp: Water Temp: Wind Speed: Wind Direction:	Air Temp: Water Temp: Wind Speed: Wind Direction:

Moon: ● ◐ ◐ ◯ ◯ ◑ ◑ ◑

Water Clarity:

Water Level: High ☐ Low ☐ Midway ☐

Fishing Rod / Reel:
Bait:
Lures:
Rig:
Fishing Method:

Notes

Species	Length	Weight	Girth

Largest Catch: Species:

Length: Weight: Girth:

Total Fish Caught:

Date:……………………….Location:……………………………….
Companions:…………………………………………………………….
…………………………………………………………………………….

Weather (AM):	Weather (PM):
Air Temp:	Air Temp:
Water Temp:	Water Temp:
Wind Speed:	Wind Speed:
Wind Direction:	Wind Direction:

Moon: ● ◐ ◐ ◯ ◯ ◯ ◑ ◑

Water Clarity:

Water Level: High ☐ Low ☐ Midway ☐

Fishing Rod / Reel:

Bait:

Lures:

Rig:

Fishing Method:

Notes

Species	Length	Weight	Girth

<u>Largest Catch:</u> Species:

Length: Weight: Girth:

Total Fish Caught:

It doesn't matter if the rod
Is or isn't bent
Time spent fishing
Is time well spent

Justin Morgan

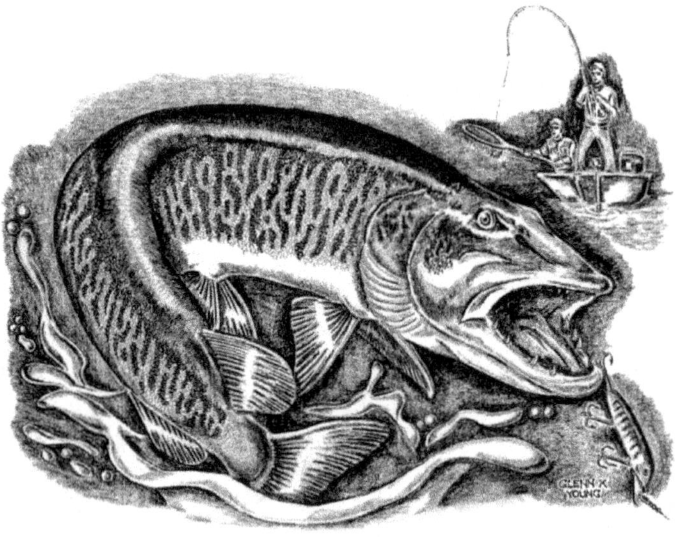

Printed in the USA
CPSIA information can be obtained
at www.ICGtesting.com
LVHW020449271123
765003LV00013B/984

9 781312 312241